Praise for *Against*

Margaret Randall's poems are written with wisdom and understanding for the complexity of life and the devious nature of history, culminating in a lyrical protest and a profound and ethical reflection on a wide range of contemporary issues. These poems restore language to its authentic meaning, reminding us of the power of words when expressing the truth, and the redeeming potential of poetry in these terrible times. *Against Atrocity* is an extraordinary poetic recounting of an exceptional life.

—Daisy Zamora, one of Nicaragua's most recognized poets, author of *La violenta espuma / The Violent Foam: New & Selected Poems*

Margaret Randall weaves sadness with possibility into a tapestry of words as she faces head-on the dangers to the earth, the realities of aging, the violence of men to women. Her magnificent poems in *Against Atrocity* push us to say our grimness out loud and then to find within ourselves humor and love and hope. She plunges into truth, carrying us into history and the future, through land and colors. Her powerful poems once again strengthen us to move forward in life, in today's world.

—Kathy Boudin, Co-Director and Co-Founder of the Center for Justice at Columbia University

Against Atrocity is a collection of poems in which historical eras flow into each other and the personal and political bleed into each other. Whether writing about incest, memory or conflict, Margaret Randall's poetry touches us profoundly because of the power of her truth and vision. In this collection, she takes us into her intimate personal spaces and thus helps us find the redemptive truth of our own private and public worlds. Hers has been a constant, powerful and steadying voice against atrocity, then—when we first encountered her writings on women's struggles in the Americas—and now, in this era of resurgence of the ethno-chauvinism of nationalisms. Margaret Randall reminds us, once again, of the power of solidarity and of humanity without borders.

—Nomboniso Gasa, South African academic and activist, author of of *Women in South African History*

Against Atrocity reminds us that poetry is never simply a set of words living alone upon the page but rather that it exists as a perennial light in the mind, as a tool of recognition that we must press into the hands of others. Margaret Randall has always reveled in the absolute agency of poetry and its uncanny ability to help reclaim our histories, to invent new forms and even to travel back in time. Reading through I was reminded of other American revolutionary poets, specifically John Trudell, D.A. Levy, Pat Parker, and Diane di Prima. In the poem, "We Are Not Seduced," Randall writes, "A bridge meets us more/ than halfway/ while a wall spans a divide/ woven of treachery." Let us read this book and rise together into a poetics of true participation. It seems the only answer back to these supposed end-times.

—Cidar Sigo, Suquamish poet and writer, author of *Stranger in Town* and *Royals*

Against ATROCITY

Against ATROCITY

Margaret Randall

San Antonio, Texas
2019

Against Atrocity
© 2019 by Margaret Randall

Cover art, "Canyon X, Arizona" © 2019 by Margaret Randall

First Edition
ISBN: 978-1-60940-605-9 (paperback original)

E-books:
ISBN: 978-1-60940-608-0

Wings Press
P.O. Box 591176
San Antonio, Texas 78259

Wings Press books are distributed to the trade by
Independent Publishers Group
www.ipgbook.com

Library of Congress Cataloging-in-Publication Data:

Names: Randall, Margaret, 1936- author.
Title: Against atrocity / Margaret Randall.
Description: First edition. | San Antonio, Texas : Wings Press, 2019.
Identifiers: LCCN 2018061578| ISBN 9781609406059 (pbk. : alk. paper) |
ISBN 9781609406080 (ebooks, all formats)
Classification:
LCC PS3535.A56277 A6 2019
DDC 811/.54--dc23
LC record available at https://lccn.loc.gov/2018061578

Note: "Against Atrocity" was the theme given to its 2019 Summer Writing
Program by the Jack Kerouac School of Disembodied Poetics at Naropa
University in Boulder, Colorado. In taking the phrase as title, I acknowledge
my debt to the brilliance and relevance of SWP.

These poems are for Barbara
who has lived them with me.

CONTENTS

COUNTING BACKWARD TO THE LAND

ART SPEAKS

SHE KNOWS

A BODY POLITIC

GOODBYE, HELLO

ADDENDA

MOVING ON

COUNTING BACKWARD
TO THE LAND

The high desert is a dog with no sense of time.*

* From "Nuevo Mexico" by Renny Golden in *Blood Desert, Witnesses 1820–1880* (Albuquerque: University of New Mexico Press, 2010).

COUNTING BACKWARD

Counting backward, common practice
at my age, I may stumble upon
the ancient turquoise bead I stooped to gather
from Chaco's purple sand.
I knew I was acting against legality
and moral rightness
when I refused to return that bead
to its millennial seasons.

Continuing to count, I might remember
a conversation pierced by shadow,
that woman who passed us on the trail,
helped when I fell against a rock,
then disappeared when we tried
to thank her: ghosts when least expected,
melodies singing in my head for years,
giving me comfort when alone.

I return to the high temperature
of steadying hands on mine
when the sound of soldier's boots
thunders through my head.
Any soldiers. Any boots. Any war.
I clutch to my breast
the birth of each child,
holding fast its place in body memory.

Counting, I always find your kiss
of prolonged intensity,
lips that thirty years on haven't ceased
to caress mine with their gentle fire.

No need to go backward
to embrace that kiss.
It is with me as I write,
bathes me in permanence.

Estimated Cost

A pleated ridge of clouds blankets my mountains this morning:
between embrace and ominous, revealing deception
normal in these times.

A hopeful young scientist proposes installing a giant fan
where it can blow frigid air off the North Pole
causing the ice cap to thicken again,

preventing a rise of oceans swallowing small nations
and the need of those whose fans are woven
of crude palm and ordinary dream.

Five hundred billion is the estimated cost for something
that may or may not work, and we all know
what estimated means.

We could decide to lower earth's temperature
by reducing our consumption of fossil fuel
but that would cut into profits

and how then would we pay for the fan? The trouble
with poets, they say, is we fail to understand
how complex everything is,

busy as we are contemplating a surprise cloud bank
and putting two and two together
in clear morning light.

CRISSCROSSING THIS GENEROUS NEST

The American bison yesterday, like caribou
or wildebeest today, Canada geese,
Monarch butterflies, and salmon
fighting their way upstream:
all follow seasonal instinct, their need
to leave and return etched in the cycle
each journey describes.

Whales swim vast miles to feed, mate
and give birth, their yearly travels
taking them along unraveling coasts
welcoming new generations
as they circumnavigate naval sonar
and other impediments
with determination that astounds.

Magnetic perception, lunar orientation,
landmarks, echolocation, scent
or solar heat:
patterns of movement handed down
from generation to generation
attract and repel whole communities
crisscrossing this generous nest.

We humans too follow patterns laid down
by need. Outcast Europeans
defying oceans to begin again in a new place,
southern Blacks moving north in search
of work and dignity.
Exploration or displacement
depending upon who tells the story.

But male need too often follows a scent
of blood: disappearance, exile, war.
The Middle Passage remembers
foul vessels stuffed with human cargo.
Today's migrations leave a trail
of deflated life vests, abandoned toys,
stories severed before The End.

Man, and it's almost always man, hungers
for war, his obsession requiring
prized properties and obscene advantage
on destruction's giant Monopoly board.
His victims have no choice but to die
while animals—our better selves—follow
the scent of sweet grass, weather, memory.

HADRON COLLIDER OF THE IMAGINATION

That towering anvil, weather with the power
to launch a flash flood
between proud canyon walls
dragging branches and bodies in its path.

Spreading up and out on this horizon
of peaceful sand and sage
against quiet blue sky the giant thunderhead
expands.

Within its fierce mystery, shards of ancient pottery
modern wrist watches
and the desperate prayers of generations
race in a Hadron Collider of the imagination.

Letters of a lost alphabet in random disarray
a manatee's desire
a million sunsets in full bloom
and fruits so rare they have yet to be tasted.

Never doubt its swirling mass hides baby birds,
a lone coyote's plaintive song
or the somersaulting questions
of someone in the wrong place at the wrong time.

THE CUP'S HANDLE

Was it burnt fingers, uneasy balance
or love of design
that led the first man
or woman
to affix a handle to a drinking cup?

When did bark and animal skins
become haute couture,
warmth and comfort cede
to this season's fashion,
an industry's grasp on our purse?

The brim of a hat addresses weather
or adds a touch of elegance,
math traces the missile's angle
or plots soil recovery,
the android heals or kills.

The moment invention claims its course,
continues to travel a river of purpose
or veers into a stream destined to run dry
on a desert where greed replaces need,
choice tells us who we are.

Or who we will be. Or even if. The switch
that diverts the tracks
is only mechanical intervention.
It cannot know where each track leads
or what will happen there.

THE RAINS THEMSELVES MAKE NO EXCUSE

Memory's deft porosity leaves tectonic tremors
on a landscape gone to seed—
every swollen arm of green
withered before the rains.

The rains themselves make no excuse, easier
to thunder through a knot of canyon
than mark time in darkening clouds
above a shifting horizon.

Repeated enough, the replacement story
clings to minds and hearts, erases
the sole of that boot imprinted on lunar dust
or how I love my daughter.

We live in a time of digital double-down
while remembering
—if we are old enough—
the pen's determined journey across paper.

EVERY OUTDATED MAP

I curl up at the corner of my living room couch,
look out the window, then quickly
look away. It is 1780, and Cuzco's plaza
is grim with rain. Micaela wails
as Tupac's body is pulled apart
by horses sent in four directions.

Conquerors from across the sea
are confident the history books
will tell the story as such stories
have always been told:
by judges standing on the sidelines,
owners of all they survey.

I go for a walk in the neighborhood and find
myself in Paris 1792. Change is in the air,
that slant of August light
and rebel voices fully aware
they are organizing a new relationship
between justice and law.

I slip behind the wheel of the old Toyota
on an ordinary Tuesday afternoon,
head to the market
where I buy the most expensive apples
because they are the ones
that taste like fruit.

It is 2017, milk bottles are thick glass once again
and I am a child. Each morning
the milkman leaves two on our back stoop
just as I momentarily reenter today's life
freed from grandfather's invasive fingers
and grandmother's predatory gaze.

On Monday I am 16, discovering the deep chasm
between desire and propriety,
what society says and what it does.
Middle of the night Wednesday to Thursday
I scrape a tabaco kiss
from the sole of one bare foot.

The elevator is broken again and José Benito
pants as he reaches our apartment,
nine floors up, two mattresses
balanced on his head.
He interrupts Doña Leandra telling me
of his death in Estelí.

Time spreads like a 19th century lady's fan
shielding from sight each mouth
that would shout the secrets if it could.
Time opens and closes about itself,
marking past, present, and future
on all outdated maps.

Every Fear Receives a Million Hits

We thrill to evidence of ancient ingenuity,
discovery of a prosthetic toe
made of wood and leather
in Egypt 3,000 years ago.

We search for solace in numbers,
Fibonacci or Chaos,
calendars that once marked our days,
Golden Proportion's dogged harmony.

Some hover in systems prescribed
by priests or gurus, easier
to follow a leader
than account for this sordid air we breathe.

It only feels like the worst time
because it is *our* time.
Holocausts and genocides also trapped
our parents in omnivorous teeth.

Headlines scream today's news and every fear
receives a million hits.
Time to acknowledge our failures
and don a cloth that fits.

EVERYTHING WE SING

Everything we sing may be lost. What was
and no longer is or never was.
A poem: eternal until someone writes it down.
This is my only time:
I am mortal, yet ignorant of my mortality.

Today when everyone may leave the same mark
I search for but do not find my face in mirrors.
I write this silence
so that some sound may contradict it
and it will discover itself: human and failing.

THE WORLD IS FLAT

An old friend tries to convince me the world is flat.
It wasn't anything she said—
metaphor making a hissing sound
somewhere between memory
and that hard edge you touch
with fingers cut and bloodied from the wars.
It is the place she inhabits
now that colors have changed places at her table.

This is the missing clue: small clouds reflected
in the glassy water of a *tinaja* or water hole
shaped by rock. Heat rising off that rock,
diminishing the water in that hole,
rendering it shallower and dryer
until there is nothing left but dust
swirling around tiny shrimp-like beings
curled into stasis until the next rains.

This could only happen upon a flat earth, not round
as the scientists would have us believe
but stretching from earliest language
to the long thin note of an Indian flute
on air that moves across the worn ropes
of a bridge sagging and ragged
over yet another body of water whispering softly
to itself. There is always another body of water

somewhere. Caught up in the round planet story—
distant poles and elastic band
at its fattened waist—
we have ignored all evidence

while keeping the terrible secret
to ourselves: a land
that moves off as far as an eye can see,
beyond all pain and reason.

The small puffy clouds remain imprinted in dust
as they once glistened on water's surface.
The flute's single note refuses to die
in our hopeful ears.
We know the rains will come
and the tiny shrimp will resume what's left
of their sixteen-day cycle. We are only who we are
right now, in this instant of clarity.

EASING MY WAY TO EXTINCTION

Industry never tires of easing our journey,
and often succeeds: frigates to horses,
stagecoach, train, plane and finally spacecraft.
Separating and reassembling our molecules
still belongs to Star Trek fantasy,
but we stake our future on invention.

The eggbeater relieved wrist action
until electric mixers stepped in
to render such effort obsolete.
Silent films became talkies, color replaced
black and white, radio gave way to television
and smaller is better in each new decoder ring.

When I learned to drive, we signaled by hand,
window down, left arm braving cold and rain.
Electric typewriters replaced their manual forebears,
then home computers arrived, delete buttons
and printers dealing a blow to White Out,
carbon paper and smudged fingers.

Calculators took the place of slide rules
which then gave way to digital sophistication.
Forever light bulbs were advertised
as ecologically sound, and recycle bins
brought civic pride. We got no-run stockings
before asking ourselves: why stockings at all?

But today's advances seem to move
to threat of panic.
Just as I've coaxed my computer
to indispensability, Apple announces
it will no longer support the programs
I've worked so hard to master.

Should I retreat to pad and pencil,
relieved not to have to learn
another technological improvement,
or simply give up, sit back and marvel
at everything planned obsolescence does
to ease my way to extinction?

MEMORY ROUNDS THE CORNER

Memory rounds the corner, wild hair
streaming behind.
She comes to a sudden stop,
unfamiliar landscape
rising on all sides.
Glaciers retreating from the heat
of lies.
Street signs in a language
she might have heard in childhood
but no longer understands.
A harvest of toys with shattered wheels.
Headless dolls.

She decides to return the way she came
but finds her path
overgrown with weeds,
fragments of words
caught in the branches of trees.
Memory tries to scratch the itch
that blooms across her skin
but there is no relief.
Then a portal of hope
beckons her tired flesh
and she follows a multitude of laughing ghosts
to a place where pain cannot survive.

ART SPEAKS

So I plunge my ear into the hollow of a black horn.
listen to it speak.
*Not one word sounds as before.**

* From "Five" by Layli Long Soldier in *Whereas* (Minneapolis: Graywolf Press, 2017).

BOOKS

I open a book and its world rises to meet me,
black and white like an old photograph
or film, where color comes
from imagination nurtured in other books
and life, places of heart or fear
reflected in mirrors within mirrors,
possibilities framed by underbrush and sky.

No head start for me. Other first-graders'
round heads found round holes while I
struggled to embrace the code that eluded,
nestled all one summer on Dad's warm lap
as he connected symbol to sound:
phonetic love.

By second grade I was ready, ready and tuned in
to protagonists who sometimes felt familiar
while others remained strangers with privileges
although I read and reread their stories.
Places too became people, real as a land
I would one day walk.

Banned books, literature a free market can accept
and those it can't, a trial where the country
of my birth ordered me deported
because of what I write: all this would come later,
not only stoking my will to read what I would,
but think and write what I must.

Today, electronic devices dominate the field,
reviews depend on what a press can spend
to advertise, the prizes fall from ivory towers
into obedient hands, and I still find solace
in my corner of the couch, turning paper pages,
sniffing the fading scent of printer's ink.

THE VERB *TO BREAK*

There's that admissible breakage
we've learned to call
collateral damage.
You can break your metaphorical back,
a child's will (never a metaphor),
sacred trust, even unjust law.

Forgive me, he grovels, *I promise
it won't happen again.*
Applying makeup to broken skin,
his wife rehearses her story,
listens to her husband's plea, avoids
his eyes already filled with future threat.

Years after her father's rage, the artist calls
her painting *Daddy Will Spank*,
refers to the child's arm in its sling
as negative space.
And yes, it was her arm.
And yes, he broke it.

One says *I'm broke* and is down a couple million
in preferred stock.
For another the same words
mean she must choose between rent,
buying food or the epinephrine pen
keeping her child alive.

When mass graves emerge across a map
of relentless war, bones shear
from other bones. Human breakage
reveals the landscape we birth
from what the verb *to break*
tells each of us.

Rendering It a Hat

How to make everyone forget who you are
by talking about it all the time.
How to make everyone remember
exactly who you are
by never mentioning it.
The it:
elephant in the room
or hidden within the Little Prince's drawing,
rendering it a hat to unimaginative eyes.
Proud, it shines upon your skin.
No one can wash it away.
Every language does it honor,
starring, finally,
as itself in the play.

Breath Carries Unwavering Meaning

I know I am asking a lot of the poem
sent out on currents of fouled air
in this time of devious deregulation.

I am aware my words may feel lonely
among so many alternate facts,
bully tweets crowding cyberspace.

What can a word do, or a series of words
strung together in urgent hope?
So much command and cliché to wander through.

But possibility explodes, pyrotechnic flowers
lighting up this deadened sky
of all-consuming rhetoric.

Mouth opens, throat clears, breath carries
unwavering meaning
through our almost silent spring.

RAUCOUS GENE AND HIDDEN HANDSHAKE

When the Golden Rectangle is found
superimposed on the footprint
of the Sun Temple at Mesa Verde
archaeologists remember Greece,

wonder that a people with no writing
or number system
replicated patterns from an unknown culture
on the far side of the world

and separated by time's vast reach.
Pythagorean triangles,
the imperial foot, a vision
that closes every circle.

When the politics of gluttony and greed
disintegrate beneath our roving feet
will such elegant images reappear
with their messages of harmony

or will we look upon this page
as evidence of life fouled,
a nightmare threatening sanity,
raucous gene and hidden handshake?

We build to inhabit, celebrate
ancestors we do not know
who left us an architecture
astonishing the eye.

May we discover an understanding
that eases our breath,
a warm breeze
to dry our premature tears.

BILL OF RIGHTS

I must make and serve the food,
we must eat the meal,
all in half an hour.
The dishes balanced on my elbows and forearms
have small wings, protrusions
that help them ride my effort.
It is my own flesh and bone
that should have the benefit of wings
but we learn well where we may borrow
the most intricate steps of the dance.

The meal finished, I look at my watch
and see only minutes have passed.
This is good news.
But I must still convince the man
with the purse strings
what works and doesn't for ordinary people.
No brandishing of terms like worker-owned
or heaven's reward.
No words whose skin has worn so thin
we pierce it easily.

I must make my case by telling the stories
passed down through generations.
But my grandparents
traded their voices for lies
and my parents were left not knowing
how to tie the proper knots.

When I invent my own stories
even dreams don't offer winning battlefields
or well-provisioned workshops, every shelf or drawer
labeled in a language I have yet to learn.

The man demands a second serving.
His appetite is running
out the clock.
The small wings,
growing from wrist to where my arms bend,
sprout claws, tiny fishhooks
placed where they catch the plot line
unraveling at my feet.
I must still make and serve the food.
We must still share and eat the meal.

ART AS HISTORY

*I believe in art as history**
she said and meant it.
Beginning hers
in Victorian constraint,
she pried it open
with fingernails described as filthy
by a family member
who couldn't see beyond
illusion's ornament.

Her portrait of Andy Warhol
with three penises
hung one above the other
—limp tower of Babel—
might today describe
any number of men
possessed by fear.

She knew about fear
pushing men
to arrogance and worse,
women to part the waters
with those tools
we've managed to save from the fire,
holding them up before us:
voracious weapons.

* Alice Neel, American painter 1900-1984.

She believed in art as history,
its power to reshape time,
reimagine the master map,
shout our greatest possibility
and most intimate pain
in a place
where we can live together.

Out of Violence into Poetry

Water, real or illusory, shimmers along
a desert horizon.
Oasis: early 17th century word
via late Latin from the Greek,
perhaps of Egyptian origin.

Egypt, a country with vast desert in which
wet and fertile exceptions
nourish life.
Also: peaceful area or period
in the midst of a troubled place or situation.

Thus, place becomes time in the blink
of geography's eye.
Embracing one another
they rise in our throats as one:
see-saw of intuition, grabbing control.

Let me satiate your thirst, feed your hunger.
Satisfy mine, if only because
we are conscious beings
standing together
in this dangerous century.

Those who see only today's power
and profit
dial the heat up, care nothing
for drought or fire.

While, powerless on the world stage,
we are reduced to small gestures:
understanding reflected in a gaze,
the touch of a hand,
oases of light where we may move
out of violence into poetry.

MADE RICH BY ART AND REVOLUTION

When I am gone and August comes
to my desert,
rain will soak sand,
its rich scent rising
to enter the lungs of another mother or walker,
someone whose intention and desire
I cannot know.

When I am gone this painting of little islands
miniature trees and birds
floating in a magical sea of cobalt blue
will hang in someone else's house.
Will that person tell the story
of poor Nicaraguan peasants
made rich by art and revolution?

A granddaughter may inherit
my turquoise earrings.
The clay pans I've used for years,
their pungency filling the house,
will offer up new generations
of bread.
Someone not yet born may read this poem.

But who will ask the questions
born of the answers
I juggle today?
Who will know the heat
of this great love
or catch fragments of my memory
reassembling just before dawn?

SHE KNOWS

she held
her slight torso
in the raw bony winter,
wearing only the smallest
*wardrobe of self.**

* From "Lighten" by Lauren Camp, in *One Hundred Hungers* (North Adams, MA: Tupelo Press, 2016).

THREE STEPS IN ANY DIRECTION

I walk past body-length mirrors holding out their seductive arms
as a megacity of young women pass, eyes straight ahead,
afraid to turn toward their own images,
fearing to recognize themselves.

The mirrors become prisons, eight-by-ten cells
where three steps in any direction
is all you get. Each women's denigrated body grows,
filling her space, punishing her breath.

I look again. Now the mirrors have become ordinary houses
where fathers weave secrets to confine their wives
and daughters, sons learn to make mirrors
look like homes.

But suddenly our streets are filled with shards of broken glass.
Legions of women have smashed the stagecraft,
reenergized bodies aiming the debris at any mirror
where secrets lurk.

The material he chooses to restrain, dominate and destroy
switches direction like boomerangs returning
to snare the bully in their traps. Something about
the master's house, the wise poet said.*

* Audre Lorde, "The Master's Tools Will Never Dismantle the Master's
House," in Cherrie Moraga and Gloria Anzaldúa (eds), *This Bridge
Called My Back: Writings by Radical Women of Color* (New York: Kitchen
Table Press, 1983).

SMILE

The first time I heard the word
was probably not as Dad
or somebody else
was about to take a picture,
recording for family memory
how happy everyone was that day.

That exhortation might have been
smile, or it might have been *cheese*
which in English lifts cheeks
and stretches lips
into that rictus of joy
advertising the perfect childhood.

Perhaps it happened earlier when,
urging her little one's expression
into a gesture that would allow her
to write "Baby's first smile"
and date the entry, Mother could be
satisfied I met all milestones.

There must be a story because today
I am reluctant to smile
at just anyone or on any occasion.
I want my smile to mean something,
blossom for a reason,
unfold in genuine delight.

For the same reason, I withhold it
when a situation requires
serious response.

There are people who will
never get a smile from me,
no matter how many babies they kiss.

EACH TIME

Each time she says *I'm sorry*, a cacophony of sound
shivers her skull. She knows that sound
and its echo. The doctor says migraines, prescribes
a pill to help her sleep.

When he calls her *stupid*, roars *don't make me punish you*
or *you're fired*, in the pit of his stomach
the voice of the man he's still trying to please
bounces off titanium walls.

A material so strong it's practically indestructible, so light
it won't allow for progress: the cowed child
radiates his pyrotechnic burst, wishes he could silence
those syllables festering beneath his skin.

Battered nerve endings drag old words, a ballast
that slows her step. A language of shame
creases the flesh of her mouth, holds her
in contempt of self.

The ditty about sticks and stones just one more
in that chorus of lies told by the powerful
to keep the rest of us in line.

SHE KNOWS

1

She knows about stairs,
how they climb
into dwellings
thinking to stay forever.

She knows about angles
—too steep
or too narrow.

The one missing step
where the big man
placed his weight
upon its gentle shoulder.

The steps where your infant head
still reverberates like a drum
after 54 years.

The corner landing,
the up
that became down.

And those stairs
that do not fit
into houses
but rise resolutely
and wander off
a knowing smile on their lips
until their heads are lost
in billowing cumulus.

2

She knows the body
cleaving in two:
new life that will take itself
beyond her borders
with or without a father's
blessing:
a human being
on its magnificent journey.

Nothing will ever be
so singular
or treacherous.

3

She knows wars born of power's greed,
won only in power's imagination,
lost again and again
on the field.

And she knows that field
is where we live
and die.

4

She knows where she is going
if not always
how to get there.

She knows what she wishes
she did not know
but only she can know

on the prickly skin
of this Socratic underbrush
its hidden surprises
lying in endless wait.

MARY WAS UNDERAGE

Well, Mary was underage—one of many explanations
meant to justify the senate candidate
accused of abusing a minor.

Forty years have passed, and now this perfect storm
of courageous women is met by men who are
suddenly forced to listen.

I remember Anita Hill facing that barrier of pompous suits,
her clarion voice overpowered by male privilege,
white and black.

He's in the crosshairs, accused by a nation of survivors
determined to tell their secrets and men who hope
they won't be next in the line of fire.

But what's this about underage Mary? Are they saying
she wasn't a virgin? Calling God a predator?
Or claiming the dogma justifying millennia

of patriarchal crime works here as well, excusing
every devout pedophile who believed
he could get away with rape?

FEMALE IT

Siri answers your questions in her even-tempered voice,
occasionally chastising you
for bad humor or language
she considers out of line.

She is the first IT with a common touch, an ordinary woman
you might say, whose forebears
—all male and worth millions—lived in gated communities
and excelled at computer code.

Fantasy gender was more fluid: embodying good and evil
(Data and Lore) or the allure
of racial mix (Deanna Troi) who sensed
what others thought and felt.

Now one has been given citizenship in a country
where women only won the right to drive
this year. Needless to say, she didn't choose
such questionable nationhood.

Will she be made to cover her body, prevented
from leaving home unescorted,
gradually melt into a landscape
of royal wealth?

Or will she rally her gender cohorts to technological subversion,
throw off the constraints of centuries
and bring equality to a land as patriarchal
as ours and almost as self-satisfied?

2020

In secret, we prepared the hundredth anniversary
of our right to vote,
passed the word from mouth to ear,
surprising those who didn't get the message
—one dead battery in a sub-scalp receptor
or faltering pulse on a wrist
exhausted by being forced to wave
when the dictator's carrot-colored mop
roared past along the Avenue.

A few received the invitation
in the old-fashioned way:
faint murmur on a hidden IPhone-12
deep in a camouflaged pocket
among the folds of her all-weather shift,
arthritic thumbs tapping the text,
calling women from every city
and holding pen,
every factory and field.

Three years since choice was permitted
the female masses:
corn rows, fuscia hair, hijab
or androgyny,
along with abortion and other rights.
All punishable now by menacing fines
passed into law on moonless nights
by robotic vote
in the only governmental chamber left.

Some of us didn't fight,
didn't believe it
a priority struggle.
Others feel skinned alive.
Now all we want is to remember.
By the time we ignored the 2018 midterms
the holding pens were full
and fully guarded,
our energy's power fizzling to fear.

In clandestine story-circles taking us back
to consciousness raising groups of old
grandmothers told the young
you don't appreciate what you have
until it's gone.
Suffrage seemed ill equipped
against all that money and influence,
fake news and alternate truth
replacing simple talk, life as it used to be.

The commemoration had
its forward agenda,
was held in a place I won't reveal
in case we must use it again.
I'll only say its eco-system
was light as air
and solid as ancient stone.
Each woman's travel
came from her ability to dream.

The dark walls of our secret place
were covered with images:
horned masks
challenging rude authority,
horses and bison from millennia past

running free in a time so deep in memory
we could not imagine
how we lived together
in its freedom.

Today on those walls we inscribed phrases
by Sappho, Coatlique,
Simone de Beauvoir, Rosa Luxemburg
Madam Binh, Malala Yousafsai
and Audre Lorde.
Someone brought an old copy
of *The Handmaid's Tale* from Canada,
and a woman from Topeka asked:
why read in fable what we live each day?

Millions exited that place, a long stream
moving as far as the eye could see,
an endless mass
of women empowered by the art
on its walls, the stories we needed to hear.
We issued forth into every street and plaza,
field and country lane,
vowing never again
to let them count us out.

Now we rise in numbers great enough
to undo the damage wrought
by these four years,
reclaim our Lysistrata place
among people bearing witness everywhere:
women
and men who offer us their honest hands,
genders that have yet
to speak their names.

On this commemoration of our
hard-earned right to vote,
joined in symbolic ceremony
with those used and abused
in every nation
on our suffering earth,
we take back what they stole
and hold it safe for those who will claim
the future we bequeath them.

A BODY POLITIC

*it is hard to move in a body so congested with
images of mutilation**

* From "Let Light Shine Out of Darkness" by Daniel Borzutzky in
The Performance of Becoming Human (New York: Brooklyn Arts Press,
2016).

AGAINST ATROCITY

For the generations that emerge from the Jack Kerouac
School of Disembodied Poetics year after year
prepared to make art against atrocity.

Against atrocity and for...
all that is not atrocity.
This is about history,
that knowledge they keep erasing
so we must start again.

Single body or mass of bodies,
fouling our habitat,
wind and fire and rising seas,
packs of rabid dogs
outbarking coexistence
all repeating themselves
where gentleness and compassion
might flourish if given a chance.

Where can we hide from the lies:
sick anthem of this century,
words turned inside out
in fear, anger, greed
and morphing to acts
because follow-through is always better
than going back on a promise,
and, you know,
We've got to finish what we started.

I want what my neighbor has:
living Monopoly board
pushing pieces from space to space

—my pieces, my spaces—
Railroads and Utilities, Income and Luxury Taxes,
Hotels, Streets, Jail—Locked Up
or Just Visiting...
Game of ideas:
unimaginable until everyone plays,
imagination gone mad.

If it is a people against their own
we call it Genocide.
If us against another
we say America First
and if a father, teacher or priest
takes what isn't his
we repeat *Our little secret.*

Secrets multiplying to plague
because boys will be boys
and men, men.
Hideous contagion spread by bloodied hands
growing from the sleeves
of monochrome suits with bright red ties,
African dashikis, Arabian thwabs,
the Sun Yat-Sen and Mao suits
or tropical guayabera:
you must dress appropriately
for such ominous command.

And men also suffer and die,
not all can live
in their privilege.
When you hurt another
it's your humanity too
gets lost,

caught among bruised nerve endings
and barbed wire's sting.

If you are in Idaho, your eye and hand
on a screen
aimed halfway round the world
we say it is easier
to escape PTSD,
cleaner and more efficient
but not for those who came
to celebrate the wedding
or dared go to school.

When they make the mistake
of getting in the way
we call it Collateral Damage:
they just happened to be
in the wrong place at the wrong time.
When no one witnesses
we lie:
so many enemy kingpins
taken out with a single strike.

Always ready to blame the victim
not ourselves,
the black kid who must have
been guilty of something,
a young girl whose skirt was too short
or woman who made her husband mad.

Don't make me hit you
he said
and you store the shame
until it burns the palm of a hand
lifted against your own child

or neighbor or enemy:
atrocity's unbroken trail of tears.

We claimed we ended a war,
saved tens of thousands
when those we called other
looked different enough,
no need to acknowledge lives,
only numbers:
tiny white birds rising in the fireball
Little Boy left behind.

A bomb to end all bombs
or war to end all wars
but wars only bring new wars,
until we can make a better bomb
powerful and precise enough
to zero in on its readymade target
carrying death
on our wings of righteousness.

We argue National Security
when internment camps
or border walls,
children ripped from mothers
who would rather lose them
to this nation of opportunity
than take them back the way they came:
sure death in the sanctity
of a threatened home.

If it's millions we call it Holocaust,
if done in a prison cell
we don't say Torture
but Enhanced Interrogation:

bright fringe or extra line of stitches
sewing the mouth shut.

If we pluck them from home or street
never to be seen again,
we say Disappearance,
unique phenomenon
making closure impossible,
a punishment lasting until
death do us part.

Atrocity of absence, presence,
language and intention,
what has been taken or imposed
curdling on
the machete's terrible edge:

Palestine
Rwanda
Sarajevo
Mississippi Delta
and Chicago's South Side
Syria's ancient stones
and modern apartment blocks
where a family of seven
is now a family of four
or one
or none.

And the child hugs his mother's leg,
eyes huge with questions
that have no answers.
The child is more because less,
pale body washed onto a beach:
focus of tonight's newscast.

For a moment the photo begs sympathy
encased in an orange vest
or clinging to her father's back,
tossed in a mass grave
or wrapped in a bit of cloth
inhabiting a box too small for death.

But death devours tender skin
dries tears
we do not understand
because they fall
in someone else's language,
switching us to automatic
as it changes our molecules.

Oh we Chosen Ones who can save
so many unborn babies
or Souls for Christ
or Wooden Indians
or Happy Slaves,
traditional families
choking on traditional pain.

Teenagers who thought they were gay
until we fucked them
like they needed to be fucked
or forced them
into conversion therapy.
She born he or claiming they
along identity's arc:
still dragged behind the redneck truck
or beaten and left to die
on a Wyoming fence.

Atrocity, atrocity: one-on-one
or one on a million:
legacy of young brides buried
alive with their dead husbands
or Hypatia torn limb from limb
outside her library.

The woman grateful to submit
to her man
her god
her place in the sun
but the sun don't shine
on atrocity,

won't shine again until
we remember
to resist the weight
of this false history,
force-fed to hungry mouths:
atrocity as heroics,
lies obscuring truth.

Good war, the oxymoron
that numbs and kills
on both sides of the aisle,
both sides of the ocean,
every side of future.

Only memory's deep breath
can turn our shame to power:
deep as an old wound,
gentle as the embrace
that excludes no one.
Welcome to
our One Last Chance.

MEMORY AS A PHYSICS PROBLEM

Tissue thin, as if pressed between the pages of a book
or vivid for some who weren't even there
but merely heard the story's echoes,
memory has become a physics problem.

I caress the images lighting my long night's sky
but other versions claim equal space,
answer the questions as they can,
solve the puzzle shamelessly.

A distant sound of war in newsflash cackle
stains plush upholstery with fear.
My father at the wheel of our secondhand Ford,
December 7, 1941.

Seven decades and we're still in that car, my child's fingers
pressed into its backseat isolation,
parents' mute shoulders shunning my pleas,
connection tumbling like dominoes.

Memory inhabits the man on the bridge or you on the couch,
your courageous fingers reaching to ignite my own,
our promise of life together born in that instant,
distance without a before or after.

The man on the bridge holds 1973 in his hands, you 1986,
my parents, long dead, 1941—or maybe not.
Translating sound and smell, voice and touch,
is the problem now.

If the survivor chooses not to speak of genocide,
a raped woman refuses to name her attacker,
silence alters memory's shape
but cannot erase its content.

Where matter and energy join loss and fire,
memory is never singular.
A current of truth parts a sea of lies,
turning all equations inside out.

No Explanation or Balance

Sometimes the best day curls within a speck of pollen
you must avoid crushing as you walk.
All but invisible to the naked eye, easy to confuse
with what is swept beneath rugs and forgetting.

Sometimes the worst day is shared by thousands
but sometimes you are alone, as knives of wind
rip the tender flesh of your cheeks,
wet with liquid loss and tired blood.

If Mengele had only observed his oath to *do no harm*,
if the stadium's guard had listened to the song
from a musician's last guitar, or 19 passengers
hadn't made it through security that day, another worst.

If the veteran cop had only taken a coffee break, parking
his patrol car instead of responding to the call
about a young Black man walking aimlessly,
hands in his pockets and, who knew?

If the husband hadn't tripped on his father's soundtrack,
if the wife had taken her child and disappeared
instead of begging *I'm sorry* one last time,
if their neighbor hadn't decided *none of my business*.

But then, oh then, if each of my children hadn't arrived,
a map of highways and country lanes awaiting
their footprints, grandchildren, great grandchildren,
obstacle courses and fresh dreams.

If I hadn't stood on that bridge, motionless in a city
where everything stopped, hadn't known
you'd come to stay, that we'd be together
all the rest of our time. The best.

The way of the world as life's seesaw rises and falls,
no explanation or balance, no such thing
as a silver lining to any cloud swollen with rain
or disappearing in a flash of light.

WE ARE NOT SEDUCED

Words, remove your masks.
Life, shelter once more
all those who breathe.

Choice, don't let them replace you
with access, pretending
everyone has it.

Fair, reclaim your legacy
in eyes and hands,
your promise.

Work, cross borders in equity,
don't tell us corporations
are human.

Post-anything will fall
on its sword
a day we least suspect.

Body mine and *body politic*: we are not
seduced as we guide memory
through this narrow door.

Female genitalia go by many names
while *pussy's* a domestic animal,
ownerless and proud.

Alternate facts are not facts
but lies. Alternate truths
wag their bodies

like tails in the narcissistic mind
of a man who shouts *democracy*
as he works at *tyranny*.

A bridge meets us more
than halfway
while a wall spans a divide

woven of treachery, sullied by words
wearing masks of deception
this or any other unsuspecting day.

"Fake News"

Dense weave of lies keeps us unsure
the sun will rise tomorrow,
darkness will comfort us tonight
or too much sugar will continue
to increase our girth
and drive our children mad.

If the showman-in-chief can tweet
140 letters of any move
he invents to bolster his trembling ego,
where may we reap truth
in those fields we've watered
with our children's tears?

Surely someone—you?—will turn
the rich earth of a restless furrow
and discover a buried root of sanity,
energy lying in wait
to help us save
the planet and ourselves.

When Good Scientists Silenced Fake News

In 500 BCE Pythagoras figured out
the earth was round.
Aristotle backed him up 150 years later.

The sun rises each morning as it always has
on this planet that orbits its mass
since Galileo gave us the news one day in 1610.

It had always been so, but alternate facts
confused our minds
until the good scientists silenced fake news.

Although some were made to recant,
sanity finally prevailed
in a future they wouldn't live to see.

Some truths bear up beneath the daily barrage
of lies and breast-beating tweets,
others require we fight harder for their claims.

Where we go depends on whether our church
rules or respects our minds,
lies or honors community.

SHOOTING THE DOG BROUGHT RELIEF

Every day to 16 his father called him
homo, sissy, no son of mine.
Then he left home.
Now when he beats the guy bloody
who looks or talks different
he feels like a man
for one brief moment.

Slut, her mother screamed, when she
got home ten minutes late,
tried to make it unnoticed to her room.
At school she whispered about the bad girls.
Now she says the bruises are her fault:
if she could only learn
to stop getting her husband so worked up.

Stupid, dumb ass, ugly: each taunt
gathered weight
as they grew,
and shooting the dog brought relief,
on the giving side now:
dispensing the pain,
passing it on in multiples.

Fear to self-loathing or self-harm,
hate speech to hateful acts
born of hate,
loner to sociopath,
crime to genocide:
no garden of Eden along that path
where love cannot exist.

LOVE IS EASIER THAN HATE

for Leymen Pérez

A poet writes about pain, uses the scraping of veins
as metaphor, evokes Vallejo:
*I do not suffer this pain as Catholic, Muslim
or atheist,*

yet Catholics, Muslims, atheists, Republicans,
and Democrats, those
who practice scripture and those
who dismiss its dogma

cause the suffering of others, deal in hate,
include and exclude
with the point of a finger, raucous
slam of a door.

Love is so much easier than hate, or at least
neutrality: *live and let live*:
muscles rest, neurons relax, blood pressure
settles in healthy rhythm.

Try it, you trumped up sycophants, followers
of the Order of the Orange Mop.
You will be
amazed.

ONE ZERO TO THE LEFT

One zero to the left, meaning left
of the decimal. Maybe it's
one of those concepts
impossible to translate.

The impact of *un cero a la izquierda*
isn't the same in English:
someone so worthless
no number can describe the air he breathes.

And then there are those for whom
even such definition pales
before reality.
A challenge no words can fill.

In any place, time or language
you can fill in the blank.
Examples abound
and the decimal stands unmoved.

I WAS BORN IN THE GOOD OLD U S OF A

When he closed my incision
the surgeon's assistant
left most of the Mediterranean
inside.

So many makeshift rafts
desperate with migrants
made it hard to sleep.

Orange vests bearing lifeless bodies
crowded my organs
and nothing worked right
after that.

A Sudanese refugee camp bulged
within my skull,
pressing against the bone
as if insistence
were the better part of reason.

I could hear myself arguing
I was born
in the good old U S of A
and only equipped
to deal with first-world problems.

But a surplus of dangerous calories
had thinned my voice.
No one heard my laments.

The surgeon and his crew
were fully insured
against such complaints.

My aging body contains
all the raw materials,
all the latest double-blind studies,
instructions and methods.
There's just no room left
to maneuver appropriate response.

HOKUSAI'S GREAT WAVE

Hokusai's great wave hung in my childhood home,
the print and ocean surge both engraved there,
delicate droplets and roaring power
suspended above an almost invisible fishing boat
as much a part of that stylized sea
as the rising foam that drew my eyes
beyond its frame.

Pure design? Modernity of form?
An image that spoke of style,
upscale calendar art
in the Scarsdale of my youth,
town where *de rigueur*
spoke a language of acceptability,
shunning low brow like the plague.

Mount Fuji at sunset might have hung beside it,
one slightly higher or lower
like the comedy and tragedy masks
in chartreuse and gold
displayed on more common walls
in homes without pretense
to such sophistication.

But then Pearl Harbor loomed in headlines,
Hiroshima and Nagasaki told as heroics
in a narrative twisted
to justify internment camps
and other shames.
Hokusai prints were no longer popular,
our honor only as good as our lies.

In my family, the far east was still the Orient,
unknown and mysterious enough
to lift my parents from tedium.
Later we bought vegetables
from Yanemoto's farm,
lovely specimens, my parents said,
and so artfully displayed.

Across the Pacific an emperor's disgrace
gave way to Kabuki masks,
a tea ceremony and the Zen
of Motorcycle Maintenance.
We avoided mentioning geishas,
praised calligraphy and acupuncture,
selective as we always are.

Until we found a new target for our need
to denigrate and spurn,
replaced bombs that vaporized cities
with U-2s and witch hunts,
loyalty oaths and more contemporary ways
of othering others
and ourselves.

A Muslim ban still decades away,
not yet imagined
by those who taught us
whom to hate and fear,
just as we cannot know today
who we will be urged to war against
in a future already imagined in violence.

No Cold Sweat in those Tropics

I cannot tell you how tired I am
of that shadowy scene,
its pieces floating through my sleep.
Always different, always the same.

Some nights it leaves off and picks up again
after I pee, just carries on as if
I'd never gotten out of bed.
At 81 there are several such interruptions
in a night.

The constant is I'm trying to get to Cuba.
There's always a hotel,
a room I lose and then find,
lots of suitcases to fill and force shut,
stuff leaking out all over the place.

The hotel is tall with many floors, a modern
steel and glass sort of place
but the elevator is gross.
A freight elevator and missing the numbers
for some floors. Maybe not even stopping
at each but in between.
Having to pull myself out, climb,
squeeze my body
into a space too small for me.

After the hotel an airport, the Cubana counter
always in the same place
just before C concourse or maybe it's A.

But between hotel and airport
there's a taxi ride, wild, not fast but wild
because time becomes liquid
and unfolds too slowly.

I'm not going to make my flight. Or I do
but don't arrive.
It's morning and I wake up tired,
exhausted from the repetition
I'm beginning to call a nightmare
even if exuding anxiety rather than fear.

I can predict it all down to the
taxi driver's gesture
and ticket agent's encouraging smile,
wind howling off the malecón,
rotting plywood
where window glass should be.

No cold sweat in those tropics,
no trembling when I awake,
only a place I no longer live that has changed
too much to be called by its name.

Exile (Details)

Dreaming, she walks from the corner of the park
to just before the old bookstore,
even when she tries to reenter sleep
wakes before she gets there,
cannot arrive.

She is born again and again,
small births and large
move each new chapter:
a Rubik's Cube
in slow motion.

Chunks of sidewalk and vacant faces
lift moments from her waking life,
wrench them from hand and mouth.
In this other place
where words bleed on her tongue,

taste flees it: pieces of a puzzle
she cannot complete.
Ketchup always an imposter
when longing for Chimichurri,
meat forever sliced against the grain.

She is reborn until she loses count
of before and after,
right hand from left,
an anthem no longer remembered
word for rousing word.

Twenty years later this nation will
still be other, and she will tire
of telling those born here
stories of the one where she used to live,
also other now.

A Longer Life Among the Ruins

They weren't of your creation, those lies
you learned to tell at 7. The world had
sharp corners and people you couldn't trust
hid behind the trees.

You honed your lies, painted sound
and color across their skin,
crafted bewitching masks at night
while others slept.

The first time you discovered an adult
you loved had lied to you,
the sky became wild and ominous,
dark clouds stopped your breath.

Once it became impossible to breathe
they named your disease, listed
side effects and offered expensive cure,
leaving you nameless and alone.

If you could not produce the requisite
number of lies each year,
you knew you would be demoted
to some century before your birth.

Now your leaders invent new names
for the lies they market and sell:
deceptive policy, eternal youth and
a longer life among the ruins.

STORIES THAT LOSE THEIR ENDINGS

Communities pulled
into lonely digits
singular among unimaginable numbers,
life jackets or broken bodies
washed ashore.

A muddy bicycle wheel
or one-armed doll
trampled by feet
whose destination shudders
through seasons of repeated want.

Language, like all such refuse,
and life itself
fall victim to this dismemberment.
In unsafe places
stories lose their endings.

War has heavy feet,
treads hard
and doesn't care where it steps,
the din in its ears
keeps human cries at bay.

We call for healing, redress,
some of us march
while others pen words of sanity
on pages ignored by those who speak
of collateral damage

as they change the channel,
tell themselves war
is human nature, after all,
inevitable
if we are to progress.

GOODBYE, HELLO

I search
for what I've lost
cannot find
*what's not there.**

* From "Manny" in *The Day of Shelly's Death* by Renato Rosaldo
(Durham, NC: Duke University Press, 2014).

BLOOD OF A POET

was the name of a film Jean Cocteau made in 1930.
Finished with opium, entering
his most prolific period, he described
a kind of half sleep
through which he wandered
as if in a labyrinth.
It lets memories entwine, he said,
expressing themselves freely.

I do not know if Eleanor Antin saw Cocteau's film
or was only inspired by its title.
On New York City's Lower East Side
between 1965 and '68
she carried a simple wooden box
that opened like a book:
laboratory slides on one side, a list
of corresponding names on the other.

If you thought there was a relationship
between the blood and the name,
she said later, *there was one.*
If you didn't, there wasn't. I do not know
what those samples symbolized
or what they mean today: relics
like a saint's thighbone or lock of child's hair?
The blood, though coursing once, fades
while the also fading names startle voice,
filling me with memory's power.

Closed, the box measures 38 by 290 by 202 mm,
open, 28 by 290 by 405.
Back then, AIDS and other plagues
belonged to a future we couldn't see
and when Ellie asked for a drop of blood
we gladly obliged, allowing her
to prick our fingers,
press them against those glass slides
and write our names on her ruled list.

Some say Allen Ginsberg was her first collaborator,
though he doesn't appear until line 61,
his beloved Peter on 63.
The first four names have so paled
they're no longer readable,
erased by the stubbornness of time.
And I think I discern George Oppen
barely legible there on 21.

Among those present though departed:
Paul Blackburn, the first of us
to leave, Marguerite Harris, Ted Enslin,
Edwin Denby, Tuli Kupferberg,
Frank Lima, Anselm Hollo,
Walter Lowenfels, Robert Nichols, Carol Bergé,
Will Inman, A.B. Spellman, and Barbara Guest:
a growing litany of vibrant spirits
now speaking only through their poems.

Lovers back then often appear above
or below one another:
George Economou and Rochelle Owens
on lines 7 and 8, I on 22
followed by Sergio Mondragón on 23,

the ink of Jack Marshall and Kathleen Fraser
touching on 43 and 44:
a record of relationships
replaced by time's unfolding.

Some names speak to me warmly:
Susan Sherman on line 13,
Lawrence Ferlinghetti on 90—
he's nearing 100 now—Ed Sanders'
haunting music, Robert David Cohen
number 91: another old lover
and father of our Ana,
or Leandro Katz
smiling quietly at number 93.

It's a digital picture I'm looking at,
not the box itself
which I haven't seen since its Sixties life.
Just as the process for keeping slides
has changed, so too communication,
and it is Facebook sends me this image
of my blood and that of others
vibrating consciousness,
filling me with rare nostalgia.

A neighborhood of poets, our names
and blood an art installation now,
owned by the Tate Modern
and loaned to exhibitions around the world.
A half century ago
we were struggling writers
happy to contribute our drop of blood
to a friend's crazy project.

Today, those still alive may be astonished
by these disappearing lines of print
and blood like ether in a changed world.
We take note of what enters a great museum
and what is denied its prestigious doors:
DNA and the names we answer to
marking place and holding time
in a history written as we carry on.

FAREWELL TO THE BIG TOP

in memoriam

The great tent is empty now, trapeze artists
fly only in our dreams and their hands
always catch the swinging bar
as they exit the picture plane.

The tiger's roar leaves a broken echo.
Elephants—trunk to tail—
no longer parade in stoic resignation
around the center ring.

The ringmaster won't crack
his long whip again
as he announces one act after another
and we hold our collective breath.

No more stale popcorn, hotdogs slathered
with bright yellow mustard, cokes
foaming above the rims
of Styrofoam cups.

The clowns have retired from their business
of laughter, hiding a sad loneliness
beneath masks of whiteface
and painted lips.

No waif in a tutu twirls on a giant ball,
no 700-pound woman
or man without arms or legs
to feed our hunger for the grotesque.

We wait in vain for a Volkswagen bug
to open its doors and release
an infinity of riders
to the crowd's delight.

Ringling Brothers has turned off the lights
in a world where wars take human limbs
and a Weightwatchers commercial
is followed by one for deep dish pizza,

a new master of ceremonies cracks his whip
in the White House and everyday life
is risky enough
to keep our adrenalin high.

A Season with No Visible Exit

You must have talked a lot
with your death...
—Juan Gelman, "Paco"*

This balmy day, air claims the word *caress*
playing across warp and weft
while sharp needles of ice
dagger my memory,
more premonition than warning.

In the bone chill cold of a season
with no visible exit,
I read *Paco* in the title of your poem
and wonder if knowing which Paco
makes a difference.

Urondo familiar in memory,
immense in tribute, huge
in a history that ended badly
but no less heroic, historic
in a time pressed close to my heart.

* From *Mundar, To World,* translated by Katherine M. Hedeen and
Víctor Rodríguez Núñez.

WHAT USE IS LOVE

For Ann Randall Beier, 1939-2017

Mom passed away at 8:11 this evening: my nephew's words
relay the death of my younger sister, awaited
but nonetheless thrusting its knife into my flesh.
A thick coat of blue, between Ocean and Azure
falls slowly over the eight until covering it completely,
while the eleven shimmers faintly: copper at sunset.

My sister's death reduces three siblings to two, changes
a balance of molecules, alters this configuration
where I've lived. Our distances erased in a single breath,
her last. Where words didn't fit before, they don't fit now.
Where we both tried hard to be friends
despite the jealousies our parents nurtured,

only love remains. But what use is love when it couldn't
do its job in life? What use words if I cannot tell
her story with mine? We no longer struggle
on a plane conceived by elders who painted our future
with brush strokes of ignorance. Too late
I touch the you-ness of you, surely a lesson there.

A poet of the north tells me his sister also died
this week. He tried to reach her side
but weather turned his plane around.
You are my sister now, he says, a message of love
bridging shared loss. *Thank you*, I respond, as I hold fast
to the blood sister gone, one strand removed

from our braided DNA. A cadmium eight turned blue
against a coppery sky. The sibling body loses a limb.
Distances recede as our story sheds its awkward verbiage.
A single fully-drawn breath settles over sisters,
one dead the other still alive, ashes of history
flying on winds that mumble our names.

Like the Perfect Poem

No peacock's dazzling display, no eagle
lifting nations
or condor floating thermal currents
above the raw rock of canyon rim.
No sweet song of the wren
or lonely peregrine nest
perched high on possibility.
No roadrunner with its trickster ways
or long assembly of crows
gathered along the telephone wire.
Neither Poe's dour raven
nor the dizzying hummingbird
whose breathless beak
laps nectar from a ready flower.
No woodpecker pecking
or cardinal brilliant against its dark branch.
No canary in the mine
or yellow descendant of that finch
who whispered Darwin's survival.
No parrot and its customary count of words,
macaw painting the jungle with its light
or quetzal of mossy mystery.
No stork tales of new life
or vulture dive-bombing to pick the bones
of what no longer lives.
No flamingo resting upon one pink leg,
no ostrich racing the Serengeti.
No frigate's puffed testosterone,
no pelican regurgitating half-digested fish
into its babies' upturned mouths.

No booby mother
teaching her adolescent to fly.

This LBJ—little brown job—
is ordinary
as an ordinary day.
Flitting low above the weeds
in any field,
it settles muted, worn,
doing nothing to claim attention
in our surround.

Yet without its generous familiarity
the web of life would be incomplete.
Without it, we might not value
the steadfast
as we do the flash of glory,
swooping in from behind
like the perfect poem.

LIFE ENDS

Maru Uhthoff, 1936-1017
Ramón Martínez Grandal, 1950-2017
Daniel Viglietti, 1939-2017

Emerging from last night's sleep
she remains dead
and they too are gone.
Maru's Tai Chi grace, Grandal's Havana images,
Viglietti singing at La Higuera
have taken their places as energy's spirit
strips memory.

Comrades are leaving in droves
and I understand
this is what happens
as life moves implacably toward its close.
Now their holograms prolong the gifts
we press to our breasts
in such elusive temperature.

If only I could touch their warm hands
once more,
live in the living breath
of all those I've loved:
hold another photograph, song or poem
to wrap me in perspective,
keep me whole.

SOMETHING WE MUST TAKE IN HAND

Daniel Viglietti: 1939-2017

His widow stood beside the coffin
as thousands said goodbye.
She opened its case
and placed his guitar beside him.

One string, broken, protruded
awkwardly.
Something always speaks after loss
even after a loss that seems

to take everything with it.
Something still carries
his precious breath, something
we must take in hand, pass on.

ALZHEIMER'S

It's not a downward spiral but a spiral
stumbling erratically
over its own feet.

You cannot hope for a better day
though against all reason
you do.

Scant recognition in eyes that once returned
your love a thousand-fold
Those days are gone.

Nights are the worst. Her internal clock
has lost its sweet rhythm,
frightened questions hover on her lips.

A friend urges to you see the glass
half full rather than
half empty.

He thinks he is helping or perhaps
cannot hold this story
in his hands.

Like another who smiles and says
she knows
everything will be all right.

The glass is always half empty now.
The half full glass lives only
in memory.

IT'S GOING TO BE ALL RIGHT

I just know it's going to be all right, she says
or he says or they say,
and I do believe they mean well,
pushing those words as if guarantees,
warranties from some all-powerful fixer,
god or statistician as the case may be.

I want to ask how they know, or by what right
they presume to toss conviction
into the swamp of my despair.
To such smug assurance I can only say
thank you, grateful I do not have to add that friend
to my current caretaker's list.

Instead I can smile and turn away,
return to the problem at hand,
my full attention on its uncertain outcome
or that certainty we do not wish
on our most ferocious enemy. I'm not about
to listen to anyone who *just knows it's going to be all right*.

GREAT GRANDSON

For Guillermo Martín Alvarez Randall,
born July 6, 2015.

He is curious, at a year and a half
pulls every book from the shelf,
turns pages, makes sounds
that are surely words,
watches and grins.

We struggle to give him a world
he can demolish, reorder
and make new, knowing
our legacy doesn't work
for everyone.

Our only option now: to bequeath
imperfection, turmoil where dis-
ease makes its faltering stand
and he forgives
the error of our ways.

Or perhaps, and I will be long gone
by then, he will write a poem
of his own to a great grandchild
he hopes may still be able
to take her desperate turn.

You Raised the Sun

For Emma Nahuí Alvarez Randall,
born November 21, 2017.

The sun came up on November 21st, 2017,
pulling centuries of life force
—radiating energy from Nahuí Ollín
to the fighting spirit
of an infant in Paysandú.

Uruguay's outlier border town
embraced its new inhabitant
struggling to survive
at 34 weeks.
Early from the womb, early to a world

challenging her in concentric scenarios:
a body trying hard to catch up
within ever widening circles
not her concern today but which in time
will require her shoulder at the wheel.

Long-fingered, well-loved, bearing a name
that opens doors invisible to most
in the interstices of space.
Emma Nahuí, you've won the first battle now,
leaving nothing on the field.

ADDENDA

sometimes a moment
is an hour, a week, a year
sometimes a decade or
a century passes in the blink
of an eye*

* From "Song for Shenandoah" by Richard Vargas in *Guenica Revisited*
(Winston-Salem, NC: Press 53, 2014).

My Tongue Breathes Fresh Air

*In December 2017, the Trump administration
prohibited the use of a list of words in a
Centers for Disease Control funding proposal.*

Waking, I found a word beneath my pillow.
Then more than one
hiding there, startled when
I slid the soft weight from their faces
and tried to still their shivering limbs.
I judged them nimble, quick at the keyboard,
full of ripe ideas.

I knew those ideas depended on my head
and also my heart,
thought of an old argument
pitting discipline against courage
as if both weren't vital
to the state of the nation
in these perilous times.

I caressed *vulnerable*, one of the words
prohibited by our Deceiver-in-Chief,
the others being *diversity, entitlement,
fetus, transgender* and *evidence-based*:
a list to test exhausted will
in this horror-house winter,
all of us simply trying to survive.

It had been a fitful night besieged
by crumbling dreams
yet those words calmed me,

whispered beloved landscapes,
a musical scale
melodious to the ear.
All very clean. No blood anywhere.

My own tongue breathed fresh air then,
rejoined the land of the living
as temperature coursed my veins
and sweat-soaked sheets.
My tongue,
naked as the rest of me,
pronounced each word exuberantly.

BOREDOM IS NOT THE WORD

On Christmas Eve, artist Carolina Falkholt completed
a mural of a massive phallus on the building at 303 Broome
Street on New York's Lower East Side, intending to stir
broad discussions about gender and sexuality. Bright pink
and very rigid, the penis stretches four stories in length, and
outraged community leaders are calling for its immediate removal.

Hyperallergic, December 2017.

What to make of the woman
who cannot get excited
by the four-story cadmium red penis
painted on the side of a building
on New York's Lower East Side?

She is not outraged, an emotion
better spent on greed or war--
has no interest
in one more display
of disembodied body parts.

Boredom is not the word, or
even *frustration*,
feelings energized in earlier times,
other worlds,
passing from memory as

we travel through the Looking Glass,
our bodies cut and bleeding,
or witness the careening glacier,
its warming slabs of ice
falling into the sea.

In my prom dress at 17
I sat on a rock--
the Jémez wilderness to my back,
arguing with my high school date
about the existence of God.

At 25 I boarded a Greyhound bus
and moved my child
beyond the known boundaries
of our universe.
New language multiplied

in my throat, filled my hands
but never uprooted
my woman's tongue,
ancient memory sewn
to palate's patient hunger.

At 47 I got my country back
without abandoning those
I'd loved along the way.
It came to meet me,
arms in warm embrace.

I remembered the entitled
football captain's reach
ripping my humiliated skirt,
and every other fear and rage
aiming to erase my words:

the husband who burned
my early poems
and the one who believed
his privilege to suggest
a proper subject for my pen.

Symbols stand and fall in line
with market whim.
Each image speaks its raucous name
or reverts to background noise
attuned to fabricated need.

I defend all body parts--flesh
or painted on a wall,
but this is about the conversations
we don't have.
Can we please have them now?

ETERNAL MESSAGE

If you've found your seat step out of the aisle
for an on-time departure
commands the disembodied voice
on this flight the airline boarded late.

Before climbing over two passengers
to get to his place by the window,
the young Cuban finds room for his carryon
in the overhead bin.

But first he unzips the duffel and points
to a plastic bag of fresh-cut roses,
three or four dozen, their petals closed
over convex centers, pink and white.

He looks around. Says something about
today being February 14th. *It'll be*
the 15th when I give them to her, but still...
He smiles, confiding his plan

to a plane full of strangers, making us all
happy accomplices.
Willing to play my part
I imagine the recipient

of this bouquet that travels to Havana
via Houston and Panama City:
fiancée or wife, sweaty cleavage
or childhood sweetheart

who will meet him at the airport,
wait while he slogs his way
through immigration and customs,
then hold out her arms

to receive the eternal message: no matter
what he did while away, or
with whom, he's all hers now,
roses and fellow travelers bearing witnesses.

BREAKFAST WITH MAX

There's that atomic clock inside the mountain,*
he says, and a man whose job
is to make sure each minute
succeeds in orderly fashion the one before.

Perfect calibration. No mishaps. Here *succeeds*
also means to succeed as in success:
working in a way that satisfies
those demigods of war and commerce.

She mentions trains: how they required
synchronized clocks to run on time,
carrying us punctually from one place
to another, one war to the next.

And I think of the Maya, unfolding
their dual calendars,
observation and imagination
shaping every future map.

My heartbeat alternates between their time
and ours, embraces the Long Count
while trying to avoid fascism's blows
to each new generation.

In the solitude of my writing space
or before the next outpost,
I decide each day
to honor Mayan imagination and my own.

* NIST, National Institute of Standards and Technology, housed in a
mountain outside Boulder, Colorado.

When she briefly leaves to add minutes to
the parking meter, we filch French fries
from her plate, rearranging those remaining
as oblivious time gains ground.

FRIDA BARBIE

A temporary injunction
delays the doll's release
as a family spokesperson decries
pale skin, insufficient body heft
and the absence
of that famous unibrow
above her penetrating eyes.

She needs more true Tijuana dress,
an abundance of jewelry
the artist wore in life—
fewer concessions to our sense
of how we demand
our doll women look.

Mattel produces stereotypes
that make us easier
to categorize and control.
No pain in the doll's face,
no broken life
surging through those plastic limbs.

The artist calls out to us
from the beyond,
demands respect
for how she lived her life,
prefers her wild frog man
to Ken's degrading company.

MOVING ON

I forget things that never happened.
And then I remember them. *

* From "Remembering 2011" by Hilton Obenzinger in *Treyf Pesach* (San Francisco: Ithuriel's Spear, 2017).

SHAPESHIFTER'S WORK

If Mother hadn't implored Father
I would have been
Margaret Reinthal,
Bat Mitzvah perhaps at 12 or 13,
accepting the liturgy
or writing a feminist Haggadah.

More likely I would have turned my back
on Jewish ritual
as I did on its Protestant clone
Mother was so sure
would erase all taint,
deliver foolproof American assimilation.

But tyranny carved early resistance
into morality's flesh and bones.
Denial wears a different skin,
sings off-key
when six million separate crimes
shadow memory.

A shapeshifter's work cut out for me,
I became the woman
who knew where she must stand
but not how to get there.
Even today, convinced non-believer,
I may trip over my own uncertain feet.

TIME'S PERFECT DUET

On Tuesday 14 minutes melted
along with spring snow
unexpected but not impossible
at the end of April.

I am missing almost two hours
that disappeared as I flew
from Albuquerque to New York.
True, the flight began at midnight
and landed at LaGuardia the following dawn.

Should I be looking at confused time zones
or hungry memory, voracious
as it ticks off each box
accounting for this blurred loss?

What of the seconds disappearing
through pleats of mind
or falling between fingertips
that only hope to dress and undress
when no one's looking?

Time like discreet views
through the window
of an old Ford.
The child believes the scenery
moves before her watchful eyes
while the landscape knows

it is the girl who will become a woman
then an old woman

and, finally, a very old woman
bringing into perfect balance

the car's speed, window's laughter,
landscape unfolding
and time's practiced duet
keeping each where it
may work its magic.

TIME'S SOUND

Time's mouth opens wide to emit
a sound we cannot hear
in the high-pitched range of dogs
or waterlogged whale-speak.
Silence engulfs us, penetrates all receptors
when it's about those hours or minutes that remain.

You may fill the wait with lurid images
or comforting sweetness,
search memory for places to hide
or leap from the lonely canyon rim.
The second hand is relentless
ticking along its ponderous journey.

Before the first child walks or talks, before
the first kiss or first consummation
of a love that lasts,
before death, when death is implacably near.
If time is meant to be a bridge
nothing can be heard

but your heartbeat, steady and reliable
until reliability too
hides in the recesses of off-map canyons,
climbs the invisible ladder
to an unseen peregrine perch where it fades
before you sense its vibrations.

TRIAGE

Meet this place where velocity creeps up on you,
takes you by surprise
and you must go this way or that
without resorting to reason.

Triage sends poison darts beneath the nails
of outstretched fingers:
who to save and who leave
to climb her final mountain alone.

Triage occupies transparency where you
come face to face with yourself
or the person you love
more than you love yourself.

It requires a new stripe on the rainbow,
a teal never seen before:
blue greener than kindness, green
that will not seek refuge in forests.

It slips and slides in its own blood,
runs circles about you,
then squeezes like a pillory for the kill,
defeating the breath in your lungs.

Choice rubs shoulders with clear evidence,
time's energy spent,
erosion's cycle clawing
at this threshold of depleted will.

Disgraced politicians or heaving gasps
of a planet battered to breaking,
morality remaining only in human hands
extended to take other hands.

Implore or let go, triage combs through hair
tangled with the sweat of centuries.
I hear you. I hold you.
I follow you to the horizon.

UNTENDED EVIDENCE

A trickle of sleep from just beside the tear duct
stops halfway down my cheek.
Ribbons in clashing colors, but really:
what colors clash?
Mexican blues and greens, oranges
and reds, have always been friends.
A thought that lifts or batters
depends upon the season.
Winter's letters cut like freshly sharpened knives.
He says he is going home
but makes a long detour: nothing is sacred, after all.
She confesses to nothing.
After all, with what she's seen
she knows *everything she writes will be used against her*
*or against those she loves.**
None of this evidence requires tending.
It grows wild
wherever you go.

* Paraphrase of two lines from "North American Time" by Adrienne
Rich.

AQUA OR TEAL

High school memories flash aqua
behind my eyes: that 1950's color
lacking the courage of teal
although teal may also deceive:
appearing too green
or distracted on a J. Crew
catalogue page.

I reject aqua now, accept only teal
as time runs out
and I claim this place
where we can speak
words that mean what they say,
hands touching living flesh,
keeping memory whole.

OVERABUNDANCE OF THE Y

*"[Echo] gazes at her desired Narcissus
but cannot initiate a conversation with
him, while he – the original 'narcissist'
– has fallen in love with his own image
in the pool."*

—Mary Beard
Women & Power

I always knew I was glad
to be female: girl
and then woman
even when all the world
saw through the male lens
and I tasted silence
in my ears.

They say you don't remember
the event itself
but the memory of the event
—ancient crime against the body—
each successive iteration
rising slightly out of tune or focus,
pale replica of the one before.

As you travel, each image
falls further
from what your body knew
eyes saw
or lips pronounced
in their struggle
to tell it like it was.

1936, and across an ocean
one war faded
while another threatened the horizon.
I grabbed their names
from between my parents' teeth
told with passion
but partial, wrong.

They could only repeat
what their parents
engraved upon their minds,
could only teach
what they'd been taught:
American exceptionalism
like male entitlement.

And I knew but didn't know
I knew.
Nazi crime cut my breath to bone
and I believed
promises like *never again*
and *moral superiority*
while across another ocean

we wrote Japan in poison ink: a place
where we could be
who we were not.
We: the eternal victors,
proud truth on our side.
They: forever othered,
sad fodder in our storyline.

History repeated those lies
in rice paddies

and underground tunnels
then down the long
American spine
and back to Africa where
origins mirror our shame.

I knew relief in womanhood
and it mattered
long before I learned
the word *patriarchy*
or identified this disease,
millennial scar
forever reopening in me.

I came home and my tongue
grew a stand of poison:
toadstools terrorized my mouth
until they took my speech
and I died again,
victim of our complicity
with the ever-ready lie.

War is always wrong.
Conquest
always pain
and children vaporized
at Hiroshima
or drowned in any migrant sea
leave the same hologram of desire,

the same unfinished life: winning
and losing, keeping
the y chromosome mighty and pathetic
in equal measure.

I knew then, and know now
but now I know I know.
And that makes all the difference.

NEW LANGUAGE

Who could have known
inventing new language
for speaking truth to power
would simply require
restoring the one we have
to its authentic meaning?

Take *revolutionary* from
the latest model car
and give it back to struggle,
erase *rebel* from fascist deceit
and it will thrive on the lips
of those who favor life.

In awe, a younger me proclaimed
I must invent a new language
for this,
seeking the words to express
what I'd been taught
existed nowhere.

Now I know it is not our use
of words alone,
but the power we wrest
and place behind each one,
fine-tuning our aim
as we sharpen our tongues.

The words our grandchildren speak
will come back to fill our mouths
in graves

from which we fertilize an earth
where only honest language
grows.

18 MINUTES FAST

That clock is 18 minutes fast, she said,
and I knew it hadn't gotten there
on its own.
No automatic speedup
but a delay her body needs
to catch up with itself.

We shape time to fit our rhythms—
breathless flutter
of the hummingbird's wings
poised above bougainvillea's brilliant pink
or deliberate tread of a tortoise
with purpose on its mind.

Just wait, we tell the young.
Too late now, the manipulator-in-chief
proclaims with glee,
unaware millennia of women
crowd his insecure flanks
in silent guard.

Time stops and takes a deep breath
knowing neither calendar
nor pendulum can keep promises
made in night's darkest hour.
Time is future now,
whetting our lips for more.

NOT SELF-EVIDENT

Riding the memory that arrived last night
were several stowaways.
We got to know one another
over this morning's granola and fruit.
One brought me news
of a great aunt on my maternal side.
Another promised questions
to troubling answers.

Etched on that memory, their exuberant wings
displayed utility on dreary days
when cold chills brittle bones
and we'd rather be anywhere else.
One spoke of the muscle
covered by plumage,
said it's important to keep it exercised
against immobility.

Inside the equation proving unequivocally
that advancing age
offers diminishing returns,
old sparks ignite new fires.
Careful not to burn my eager fingertips
I let my arms fall to each side,
refusing to fold them across my breast
in defensive iconography.

Within this complex harmony
my battered ears record
I hear the whisper of old stories,

view images passing slowly
before my dimming eyes,
hold these truths to be,
if not self-evident,
powerful for whatever time remains.

THE COMMON EDGE

Pieces of a three-dimensional puzzle
we humans learn this indentation
fits that protrusion, curves and corners
moving into and against one another,
vulnerability meeting compassion
or fear's sharp edge receiving
the tender touch intended
for those secrets burdened by our lies.

Years searching for the common edge,
contact dissolving along a line
where humanity may soothe
answers and also questions, a place
of our making, song to be sung
in a language we can never fully probe.
Its surprises link our hands
in commitment or beyond.

Conscious of how we move into
or away from each other,
conscious or not of what we bring
to that moving line, we etch
boundaries on a map that mirrors
such partial image of self.
Here today, gone tomorrow, we leave
to our children this faltering narrative of place.

ACKNOWLEDGMENTS

Several of these poems, sometimes in earlier versions, appeared first in *About Place Journal*, *Erizo* (Mexico City), *Poetry Ink*, *So It Goes* (Kurt Vonnegut Library Journal), *SWP Guerilla Lit Mag*, *Taos Journal of Poetry*, *Trumped: Poets Speak (While They Still Can)*, *Visible Binary #3*, *Fixed & Free Anthology*, *Revista Casa de las Américas* (Havana, Cuba), and two special chapbooks, one dedicated to the work of South African poet Dennis Brutus and myself and the other honoring Sonia Sánchez, both published by Moonstone in Philadelphia. A few were included in the final, as yet uncollected in book form, section of *Time's Language: Selected Poems 1959-2018* (also published by Wings). As always, I want to express my deepest gratitude to Bryce Milligan, who has curated my poetry since 2009.

ABOUT THE AUTHOR

Margaret Randall is a feminist poet, writer, photographer and social activist. She is the author of over 100 books. Born in New York City in 1936, she has lived for extended periods in Albuquerque, New York, Seville, Mexico City, Havana, and Managua. Shorter stays in Peru and North Vietnam were also formative. In the 1960s, with Sergio Mondragón she founded and co-edited *El Corno Emplumado / The Plumed Horn,* a bilingual literary journal which for eight years published some of the most dynamic and meaningful writing of an era. Robert Cohen took over when Mondragón left the publication in 1968. From 1984 through 1994 she taught at a number of U.S. universities.

Randall was privileged to live among New York's abstract expressionists in the 1950s and early '60s, participate in the Mexican student movement of 1968, share important years of the Cuban revolution (1969-1980), the first three years of Nicaragua's Sandinista project (1980-1984), and visit North Vietnam during the heroic last months of the U.S. American war in that country (1974). Her four children—Gregory, Sarah, Ximena and Ana—have given her ten grandchildren and two great-grandchildren. She has lived with her life companion, the painter and teacher Barbara Byers, for the past 33 years.

Upon her return to the United States from Nicaragua in 1984, Randall was ordered to be deported when the government invoked the 1952 McCarran-Walter Immigration and Nationality Act, judging opinions expressed in some of her books to be "against the good order and happiness of the United States." The Center for Constitutional Rights defended Randall, and many writers and others joined in an almost five-year battle for reinstatement of citizenship. She won her case in 1989.

In 1990 Randall was awarded the Lillian Hellman and Dashiell Hammett grant for writers victimized by political repression. In 2004 she was the first recipient of PEN New Mexico's Dorothy Doyle Lifetime Achievement Award for Writing and Human Rights Activism.

Recent non-fiction books by Randall include *To Change the World: My Life in Cuba* (Rutgers University Press), *More Than Things* (University of Nebraska Press), *Che On My Mind,* and *Haydée Santamaría, Cuban Revolutionary: She Led by Transgression* (both from Duke University Press). Her most recent nonfiction works are *Only the Road / Solo el Camino: Eight Decades of Cuban Poetry* (Duke, 2016) and *Exporting Revolution: Cuba's Global Solidarity* (Duke, 2017).

"The Unapologetic Life of Margaret Randall" is an hour-long documentary by Minneapolis filmmakers Lu Lippold and Pam Colby. It is distributed by Cinema Guild in New York City.

Randall's most recent collections of poetry and photographs are *Their Backs to the Sea* (2009), *My Town: A Memoir of Albuquerque, New Mexico* (2010), *As If the Empty Chair: Poems for the Disappeared / Como si la silla vacía: poemas para los desaparecidos* (2011), *Where Do We Go from Here?* (2012), *Daughter of Lady Jaguar Shark* (2013), *The Rhizome as a Field of Broken Bones* (2013), *About Little Charlie Lindbergh and other Poems* (2014), *Beneath a Trespass of Sorrow* (2014), *Bodies / Shields* (2015), *She Becomes Time* (2016), and *The Morning After: Poetry and Prose in a Post-Truth World* (2017), all published by Wings Press. In October of 2017, she was awarded the prestigious Medal of Literary Merit by Literatura en el Bravo, Chihuahua, Mexico. *Time's Language: Selected Poems (1959-2018)* was published by Wings Press in 2018.

WINGS PRESS

COLOPHON

This first edition of *Against Atrocity*, by
Margaret Randall, has been printed on 55
pound "natural" paper containing a percent-
age of recycled fiber. Titles have been set in
Chaucer, Chalkdust, and Lithos Pro type, the
text in Adobe Caslon type. This book was
designed by Bryce Milligan.

On-line catalogue and ordering:
www.wingspress.com
Wings Press titles are distributed to the trade by the
Independent Publishers Group
www.ipgbook.com
and in Europe by Gazelle
www.gazellebookservices.co.uk

Also available as an ebook.

*For more information about Margaret Randall,
visit her website at www.margaretrandall.org.*